PEOPLE IN MY NEIGHBORHOOD

THE WASTE COLLECTOR

Jared Siemens

LIGHTBOX
openlightbox.com

LIGHTBOX

Go to
www.openlightbox.com
and enter this book's
unique code.

ACCESS CODE

LBXD6795

Lightbox is an all-inclusive digital solution for the teaching and learning of curriculum topics in an original, groundbreaking way. Lightbox is based on National Curriculum Standards.

OPTIMIZED FOR

- ✓ **TABLETS**
- ✓ **WHITEBOARDS**
- ✓ **COMPUTERS**
- ✓ **AND MUCH MORE!**

STANDARD FEATURES OF LIGHTBOX

AUDIO High-quality narration using text-to-speech system

VIDEOS Embedded high-definition video clips

ACTIVITIES Printable PDFs that can be emailed and graded

WEBLINKS Curated links to external, child-safe resources

SLIDESHOWS Pictorial overviews of key concepts

INTERACTIVE MAPS Interactive maps and aerial satellite imagery

QUIZZES Ten multiple choice questions that are automatically graded and emailed for teacher assessment

KEY WORDS Matching key concepts to their definitions

VIDEOS

WEBLINKS

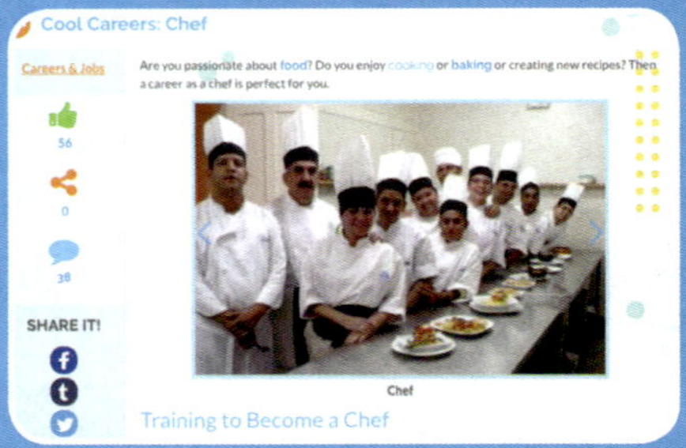

SLIDESHOWS

QUIZZES

PEOPLE IN MY NEIGHBORHOOD

THE WASTE COLLECTOR

There are many different people in my neighborhood.

The waste collector is a person in my neighborhood.

Waste collectors start their day at a landfill or recycling center.

These are places where waste is sent after it is collected.

A waste collector gathers waste from people's homes.

More than **68,000 people** work as **waste and recycling collectors** in the United States.

Waste collectors may gather garbage, recycling, or food waste.

Waste collectors often work in teams. One person drives a large waste truck.

One or two other people load waste into the back of the truck.

A waste collector may run **20 miles** (32 kilometers) behind a waste truck **each day**.

Waste collectors wear safety boots and glasses. They wear bright vests that reflect light.

These vests help drivers and other cars to see them while they are putting waste in the truck.

Waste trucks have a special tool that squishes waste. This makes it smaller.

This means the waste collector can gather more trash before going back to the landfill.

Some waste collectors work alone. Their trucks have a robot arm.

This arm can pick up waste bins and dump them into the truck.

Waste collectors help keep my neighborhood clean.

They help make my city a place people want to visit.

New York City makes **more garbage** than **any other city** in the world.

Waste collectors are important people in my neighborhood.

Each person in the United States makes about **4.4 pounds** (2 kilograms) of trash **each day**.

See what you have learned about the waste collector.

Describe what you see in each of the pictures.

KEY WORDS

Research has shown that as much as 65 percent of all written material published in English is made up of 300 words. These 300 words cannot be taught using pictures or learned by sounding them out. They must be recognized by sight. This book contains 66 common sight words to help young readers improve their reading fluency and comprehension. This book also teaches young readers several important content words, such as proper nouns. These words are paired with pictures to aid in learning and improve understanding.

Page	Sight Words First Appearance
4	are, different, in, many, my, people, there
5	a, is, the
6	at, day, or, start, their
7	after, it, places, these, where
8	and, as, from, homes, more, states, than, work
9	food, may
10	large, often, one
11	back, each, into, miles, of, other, run, two
12	light, that, they
13	cars, help, see, them, to, while
14	have, makes, this
15	before, can, means
16	some
17	up
18	keep
19	any, city, new, want, world
21	about, important

Page	Content Words First Appearance
4	neighborhood
5	person, waste collector
6	landfill, recycling center
7	waste
8	United States
9	garbage, recycling
10	teams, waste truck
12	boots, glasses, vests
13	drivers
14	tool
15	trash
16	robot arm
17	bins
19	New York City

Published by Smartbook Media Inc.
350 5th Avenue, 59th Floor New York, NY 10118
Website: www.openlightbox.com

Library of Congress Control Number: 2018930440

ISBN 978-1-5105-3823-8 (hardcover)
ISBN 978-1-5105-3824-5 (multi-user eBook)

032018
120117

Printed in Brainerd, Minnesota, United States
1 2 3 4 5 6 7 8 9 0 22 21 20 19 18

Project Coordinator: Jared Siemens
Designer: Nick Newton

Every reasonable effort has been made to trace ownership and to obtain permission to reprint copyright material. The publisher would be pleased to have any errors or omissions brought to its attention so that they may be corrected in subsequent printings.

The publisher acknowledges Alamy, Getty Images, and iStock as its primary image suppliers for this title.